My First Communion

Dorothy Haas
photographs by Wm. Franklin McMahon

Albert Whitman & Company, Niles, Illinois

Library of Congress Cataloging-in-Publication Data

Haas, Dorothy F.
    My first communion.

    Summary: Describes a Catholic girl's preparations
for her First Communion, the ceremony itself, and her
celebration afterwards with her family.
    1. First communion—Juvenile literature. 2. First
communion—Pictorial works. 1. [First communion]
I. McMahon, William Franklin, ill. II. Title.
BX2237.H33 1987   264'.02036   86-18892
ISBN 0-8075-5331-X (lib. bdg.)

Text ©1987 by Dorothy F. Haas
Photographs ©1987 by Albert Whitman & Company
Published in 1987 by Albert Whitman & Company, Niles, Illinois
Published simultaneously in Canada by General Publishing, Limited, Toronto

Design by Meyer Seltzer

Remembering my brother Father Robert Haas. D.H.

To Debby and her cooperation on projects like this. W.F.M.

My name is Claire Marie. I'm eight years old. I play soccer, and I'm learning to ski. But what I like best is rollerskating. I like to feel my skates rolling smoothly or thumping over the cracks. The wind cools my face, and the new leaves on the trees smell sweet.

I wish my friend Melanie still lived here. We're very best friends. We used to play together and tell each other our secrets. But Melanie moved far away.

If Melanie still lived near me, we could skate together.

If Melanie was here, we would be in the same First Communion class.

My sisters and brother and I all have jobs to do at home. I help set the table for meals and clear up afterward. Most of the time we use our everyday dishes. But when company comes, we use Mom's prettiest dishes. We put flowers on the table and light candles. Then we know someone special is coming to eat with us.

Another one of my jobs is studying. Mom says that's my biggest job right now.

I go to Our Lady of Perpetual Help School. I'm in second grade. Second grade is lots harder than first grade. You read harder books. You do harder math. And if you're Catholic, you learn all the things you need to know to make your First Communion.

I'm going to make my First Communion soon. Our class has been studying all winter.

Every day Mrs. Cadwell, our teacher, reads stories from the Bible to help us understand about First Communion. There are many stories about Jesus sharing food with people.

Philip likes the story of the loaves and fishes. There's a boy in that story.

I like the story of the wedding feast at Cana. I think the bride must have been pretty.

Sometimes we color Bible story pictures and cut them out. Marianne and I share our crayons.

Last week we all wrote letters to Jesus. We told him how we feel about First Communion. I didn't tell anyone what was in my letter. It's a secret between Jesus and me.

I study at home every day after school. Mom listens to me say my prayers to be sure I know them. We talk about what the words in the Our Father mean. Mom says that another name for the Our Father is the Lord's Prayer.

My little sister, Moira, is just learning to say her prayers. I teach her how to make the sign of the cross.

I make a banner about Communion, too. I make it all by myself. Mom puts it on the dining-room table where everyone can see it.

Sometimes Daddy helps me study. We talk about making my First Communion and what Communion means. It means that Jesus is truly with us in the bread and wine at Mass.

My big sister Sarah says it means, too, that in sharing the bread and wine we come closer to Jesus and each other.

My sister Laura says it means we are supposed to carry Jesus' love to everyone when we leave church.

Mrs. Cadwell says that Communion is a meal we all share. It's like eating with our friends.

Sometimes Mom and Daddy eat with their friends. They ask them to come to dinner.

Melanie and I are friends. We used to eat at each other's houses.

Jesus ate with his friends on the last night he spent on earth. They shared bread and wine. People call that the Last Supper. It was the very first Communion.

We practice how to act in church on First Communion day. We sing. We set the table for our Communion meal. We carry flowers and candles to the altar to make it beautiful.

Some of us practice talking into the microphone. We must speak loud and clear.

When we finish practicing, Tony and I lead everyone out of church. We go first because we are the shortest boy and girl in our class.

I think my First Communion day will never come. But it does. It's today. I'm so excited I wake up when the sun comes up. The house is so still I can hear my clock humming. I write a poem about humming clocks in my diary. I write about the sky, too. It's full of pink and yellow streaks.

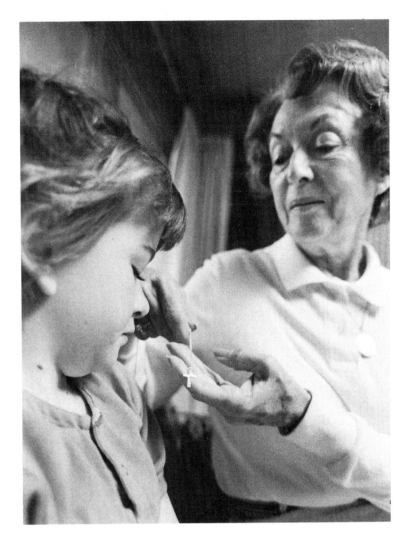

After a while I go looking for someone to talk to.

My grandmother and grandfather have come all the way from California for my First Communion. Nana is awake. She gives me a gold cross on a chain. It's the prettiest cross I have ever seen.

When it's time to get dressed, Mom helps me. I'm the ninth girl in my family to wear this dress. It's thirty-eight years old. We have a picture of Mom in the same dress! She wore it for her First Communion. Her sisters wore it. Sarah and Laura wore it. Someday Moira will wear it. I wonder who will wear it after that.

At church, we wait in the basement until everyone comes. Mrs. Cadwell is here. So are the other second-grade teachers. They remind us not to forget things. And we sing our songs one more time.

I feel full of waiting—and shy, too. Everyone is going to look at Tony and me when we walk into church. Mom says it's okay to feel shy—sometimes that's the way we get ready to do hard things.

At last we line up at the back of the church. Everyone is here except Robbie. Robbie has chicken pox. We all feel sad for him.

The organ starts to play. Tony and I walk into church and everyone follows us. I look straight ahead. Only, just once, I peek at Mom and Daddy.

We do everything just the way we practiced. We sing. We tell the story of Moses in the desert and how God fed the people when they were hungry.

When it's time to get the altar ready for our Communion meal, the boys in the honor guard stand at the steps. The things we need are on a table nearby.

So that everyone in church will understand, some of us explain what our classmates are doing. They put the cloth on the altar. They bring candles and baskets of flowers. They bring the letters we wrote to Jesus.

I wait a long time to say my part. I wonder if I'll speak loud enough. What if I stumble on the words! What if I hiccup!

When it's my turn, I say, "At the Last Supper, Jesus had bread and wine. He prayed over this food and gave it to his friends. That's why we bring bread and wine to our table."

When I finish, I give a big sigh. I didn't stumble on the words. I didn't hiccup.

Servers help at the altar. They light candles and bring the big prayer book to the priest. My brother Chris is a server today.

Father Sullivan prays. He holds up the bread and says the words Jesus spoke at the Last Supper. "Take this, all of you, and eat it. This is my body." Then he holds up the cup of wine and says, "Take this, all of you, and drink from it. This is the cup of my blood, the blood of the new and everlasting covenant. It will be shed for you and for all so that sins may be forgiven. Do this in memory of me."

After that we all say the prayer Jesus taught us, the Lord's Prayer. We hold hands while we pray.

At last it's time for Communion, my First Holy Communion. We stand in a circle in front of the altar. I feel all still inside. Jesus is really coming to me.

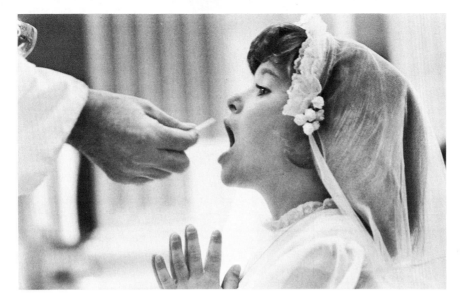

Father Sullivan puts the bread on my tongue.

Then I go back to my seat. I think about Jesus. I say a prayer I wrote. Here's part of it: "Thank you for coming to me, Jesus. Thank you for being my friend. Help us all to love one another."

From now on, when I go to Mass, I can receive Communion just the way grownups do. I will take the bread in my hand and put it in my mouth myself. And I can drink wine from the cup.

Everyone smiles at us when we walk out of church. Sarah takes my picture. Laura waves at me. I smile at them. I'm proud and happy—and almost grown up.

Mom and Daddy have invited our family and friends to lunch after church. There are lots of presents. My sisters watch me open them. So do my friend Kelly and her little sister.

There's a prayer book from Mom and Daddy and a necklace from Katie and Mary. And guess what! There's even a present from Melanie.

Melanie wrote me a letter, too. She says she's going to make her First Communion next Sunday. She's not going to be part of a class, though. She's going to receive Communion at Mass with her family.

I guess there are lots of ways of making your First Communion. My friend Katie and her brothers did it at home, with just their family. Their little sisters Mary and Colleen will do that, too.

Last of all, we sit down to eat together. People who love each other like to share meals. There's a pretty cloth on the table. There are flowers. There's chicken—and fruit salad and ice cream. And no brussels sprouts! And my banner is right in the middle of the table for everyone to see.

After dinner, the grownups sit and talk...and talk...and talk.
But the rest of us do what we like to do best—we play games.

I think I will remember my First Communion day for ever and ever.

Dorothy Haas writes for children, she says, because it's more fun than anything else she might do. She works in her Chicago high-rise apartment overlooking Lincoln Park and Lake Michigan and has used her neighborhood as a setting for several books, including *Poppy and the Outdoors Cat* and *Tink in a Tangle*, novels about two lively little girls. *Tink* was selected by the editors of the American Library Association's *Booklist* as one of the best children's books of 1984. Miss Haas is also an editor, and during her career she has been responsible for the publication of more than six hundred books.

In 1979 Dorothy Haas received the Children's Reading Round Table Award for distinguished service in the field of children's literature.

Frank McMahon takes photographs for children's books, for magazines such as *Time* and *People*, and for corporations including Sears and IBM. His work has taken him to Canada, Mexico, and England as well as all around the United States. Mr. McMahon's photographs have won awards in journalistic and corporate competitions.